What's So Bad About GASOLINE?

Fossil Fuels and What They Do

By Anne Rockwell

Illustrated by Paul Meisel

Collins
An Imprint of HarperCollinsPublishers

Special thanks to Mark A. Cane, G. Unger Vetlesen Professor of
Earth and Climate Sciences, Lamont-Doherty Earth Observatory
of Columbia University, for his valuable assistance.

The Let's-Read-and-Find-Out Science book series was originated by Dr. Franklyn M. Branley, Astronomer
Emeritus and former Chairman of the American Museum–Hayden Planetarium, and was formerly
co-edited by him and Dr. Roma Gans, Professor Emeritus of Childhood Education, Teachers College, Columbia
University. Text and illustrations for each of the books in the series are checked for accuracy by an expert in the
relevant field. For more information about Let's-Read-and-Find-Out Science books, write to HarperCollins Children's
Books, 1350 Avenue of the Americas, New York, NY 10019, or visit our website at www.letsreadandfindout.com.

Library of Congress Cataloging-in-Publication Data
Rockwell, Anne F.
What's so bad about gasoline? : fossil fuels and what they do / by Anne
Rockwell ; illustrated by Paul Meisel.—1st ed.
p.   cm. — (Let's-read-and-find-out science. Stage 2)
ISBN 978-0-06-157527-3 (pbk.) — ISBN 978-0-06-157528-0 (trade bdg.)
1. Gasoline—Juvenile literature.   2. Fossil fuels—Juvenile literature.
3. Carbon dioxide—Juvenile literature.   I. Meisel, Paul, ill.   II. Title.
TP692.2.R63 2009   2007052947   665.5'3827—dc22   CIP   AC
Typography by Rachel Zegar
1 2 3 4 5 6 7 8 9 10

First Edition

For the starting-to-drive
members of my family
—A.R.

For all kids who are concerned
about the future of our planet
—P.M.

We go to the gas station and fill up the tanks of our cars, and we're ready to go. Anywhere, everywhere! In big cars, small cars—all kinds of cars. Gasoline is what makes cars go.

What is gasoline, anyway?

Gasoline is a kind of fuel. When it's burned, it gives engines power. But carbon dioxide, other gases, and small particles of ash go into the atmosphere as the fuel burns. These are called emissions.

The engine burns fuel.

Muffler

Gas Tank

Carbon dioxide is a gas that traps heat above the earth's atmosphere. Too much carbon dioxide in the atmosphere makes the earth warmer than it should be. We call this global warming.

Sun

Carbon Dioxide released into the atmosphere creates a greenhouse effect.

The planet's heat gets trapped.

Every year more and more people all over the world drive cars. And every year the earth grows warmer.

Gasoline is made from petroleum, which is a fossil fuel. Fossils are what remain of plants and animals that lived millions or billions of years ago. Maybe you've seen some in stone. You can't see the ones that make petroleum, for they are too tiny, but they are there.

Stone with leaf fossil.

Microscopic Algae

Long ago, tiny plants and animals lived in oceans that covered much of the earth. When these plants and animals died, they drifted down to the ocean floor. As millions of years passed, they became covered with sand. As more time passed, the sand turned to rock.

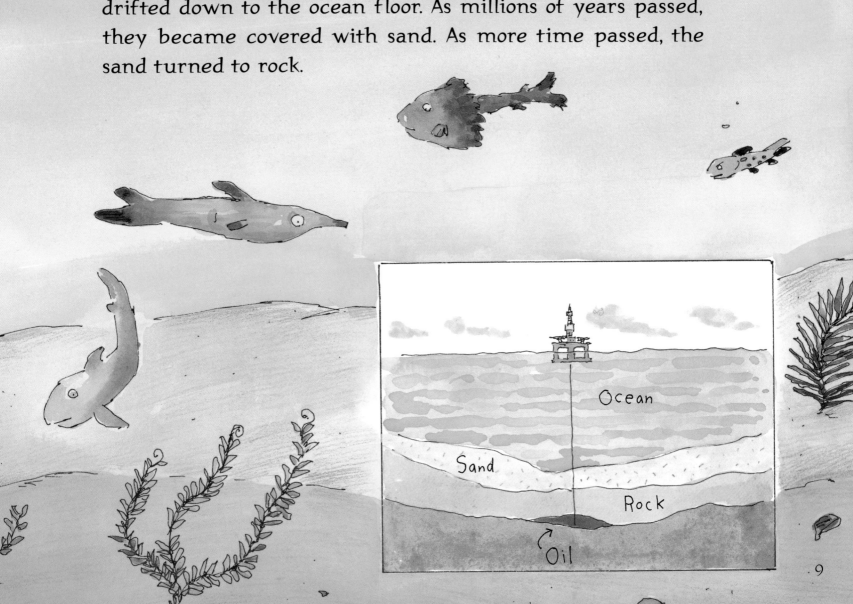

Ocean

Sand

Rock

Oil

9

The decaying matter from the tiny plants and animals was trapped beneath the rock. This trapped decaying matter changed into petroleum. Some of the oceans dried up and left huge petroleum deposits deep underground. Some petroleum remained under the water of the ocean. These deposits under land or sea are where we get petroleum, or crude oil, to make gasoline.

11

People knew about petroleum long ago. There is more in the Middle East than anywhere else in the world. In the sandy deserts of those lands, people sometimes found sand that was moist and oily. Petroleum had seeped up through the ground. They used this oily material to waterproof boats, to preserve mummies, or to rub on their dry skin. They never tried to dig up more because they didn't need to. They didn't use much. Petroleum is still used today to make skin lotions.

Bitumen is thickened petroleum that is still used in road paving. Ancient builders used it to strengthen bricks and in the mortar that held bricks and stones together.

Two thousand years ago, Arabians took baths in petroleum oil and water that they thought strengthened their bodies.

The first oil wells were drilled in China during the fourth century. Wells dug with a bamboo pole could reach depths of eight hundred feet.

The distilling process was discovered in the eighth century. Distilling changes a chemical substance into something else. When a liquid chemical substance is heated to the boiling point, a new kind of liquid is given off. This is called a distillate.

In the nineteenth century, people discovered they could make kerosene out of distilled petroleum. Kerosene was a very useful distillate. People lit lamps with it and burned it in stoves to keep warm. But they still didn't use much petroleum.

Everything changed when the automobile was invented in the late nineteenth century. Then petroleum became very useful. It could be distilled into gasoline, which made cars go far and fast. It worked better in car engines than kerosene did. Gasoline was cheap and there seemed to be plenty of the crude oil needed to make it if people dug deep enough in the right places.

People began digging and digging deeper and deeper to find deposits of petroleum. They learned how to put floating oil rigs out in the ocean to drill holes and pump it from under the seafloor.

As people dug and pumped more and more crude oil, they made more and more gasoline in oil refineries.

Refineries are where crude oil is distilled into gasoline. Gasoline became plentiful, making it possible for more and more people to drive their own cars—not to mention tractors, lawn mowers, motorboats, and other gas-powered vehicles to make life easier, or even more fun.

Swamps from
250 million
years ago

Another kind of fossil fuel is coal. Coal is not a liquid fuel like petroleum but solid like a rock. It is not made from microscopic plants and animals. Instead it is made from plants that once grew in huge swamps that covered the earth. We dig it out of the earth in coal mines and burn it to heat homes and make machines work. Some of these machines make the electricity we use; some help people make things in factories. But burning coal also puts a lot of carbon dioxide and other emissions into the atmosphere.

There is a bad thing about this. Fossil fuels such as gasoline and coal emit more carbon dioxide than any other kind of fuel.

They make so much carbon dioxide because they are made of carbon. Carbon is part of every living thing. We are made of carbon.

So are the plants that grow in our yards and the birds and insects that live in them. When you burn carbon, it burns long and hot, but because it is made from living things, or organic matter, not all of it burns. Partially burned carbon pollutes the air we breathe. It makes it dirty.

And *every* year the people of the world burn more fossil fuel.

More and more carbon dioxide traps more and more heat above the earth's atmosphere. Scientists who study the earth and the environment now think the warmer air makes glaciers and polar ice caps melt. Sea levels rise. Shorelines and islands shrink. Many plant and animal species cannot live in the places they always have. The world is changing, and the changes aren't good.

One day there won't be any more petroleum. It will all be used up. When it's gone, we won't be able to make any more because it was made by nature billions of years ago. It took a long time for the prehistoric plants and animals that died to turn into coal and petroleum.

If people keep using these fuels, a lot more damage will be done to all living things on the earth. For nothing does more damage to the atmosphere than burning fossil fuels.

We need to find other ways to get the fuel we need. We have to find ways to use less, too. And we need to find these things soon.

Fortunately there are other ways—if we're smart enough to think of them and willing to change our habits.

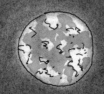

We can harness and store power from the sun to make machines go. We can use windmills to harness and store power from wind. We can use nuclear energy. We can capture and store energy from waves and tides in the ocean. We can even capture emissions from factory chimneys and recycle them. That way they don't go up into the atmosphere. We can make other kinds of automobile fuel from corn, wheat, soybeans, or sugarcane, or even water. These fuels do not put as much carbon dioxide into the atmosphere as gasoline does.

It's important that we all figure out ways not to depend on fossil fuels. Because this planet belongs to all of us, all of us need to take care of it.

What ways can you think of to help?

Find Out More About
GASOLINE

- Across the earth, about 83 million barrels of crude oil are produced a day and about 83 million barrels of oil are consumed a day.

  (www.eia.doe.gov/oiaf/ieo/oil.html)

- There are 42 gallons of crude oil in a barrel. One barrel of oil can produce 19.6 gallons of gasoline.

  (http://tonto.eia.doe.gov/ask/gasoline_faqs.asp#gallons_per_barrel)

- The United States consumes about 400 million gallons of gasoline a day!

  (http://auto.howstuffworks.com/question417.htm)

- That equals 146 billion gallons of gasoline a year! That's more than any other country consumes.

  (http://auto.howstuffworks.com/question417.htm)

- Through this incredible consumption of gasoline, the United States is releasing roughly 2 billion pounds of carbon into the atmosphere every day!

  (http://auto.howstuffworks.com/question417.htm)

- Current estimates say that there are approximately 2 trillion barrels of oil left in the world.

  (www.pr.caltech.edu/periodicals/caltechnews/articles/v38/oil.html)

Top 5* Oil Exporters
(where the oil comes from):
1. Saudi Arabia
2. Russia
3. Norway
4. Iran
5. United Arab Emirates

Top 5 Oil Importers
(where the oil goes):
1. United States
2. Japan
3. China
4. Germany
5. South Korea

Top 5 Oil Consumers
(who uses the most oil):
1. United States
2. China
3. Japan
4. Russia
5. Germany

These are the most common uses for one barrel of crude oil by percentage. (Percentages equal more than 100 because of an approximately 5% processing gain from refining.)

47% gas for cars
23% heating oil and diesel fuel
18% other products
10% jet fuel
4% propane
3% asphalt

(http://tonto.eia.doe.gov/ask/gasoline_faqs.asp)

* "Top 5" information comes from
www.eia.doe.gov/emeu/cabs/topworldtables1_2.htm.

33